PANAMA CANAL

by M. C. Hall

ROURKE PUBLISHING
Vero Beach, Florida 32964

www.rourkepublishing.com

Photo credits: AP Images, cover, 30, 39, 40, 45 (top), 45 (bottom); iStockphoto, cover, 5, 11, 17, 23, 29, 37; North Wind Picture Archives/Photolibrary, 4, 7 (left), 13 (left), 15 (left), 22, 42 (top); Art Media/Photolibrary, 7 (right), 42 (bottom); Library of Congress, 8, 10, 13 (right), 16, 19 (top), 21 (right), 25 (left), 25 (right), 27, 31, 42 (second from bottom), 43 (top), 43 (bottom), 44 ; Bettmann/Corbis, 15 (right); Harris & Ewing/Library of Congress, 19 (bottom), 21 (left), 42 (second from top); Andoni Canela/Photolibrary, 29; Chris Forsey/Dorling Kindersley, 35 (top); Dorling Kindersley, 35 (bottom); Jane Sweeney/Photolibrary, 36; Corbis, 33, 38; Erwin Bud Nielsen/Photolibrary, 41

Editor: Melissa Johnson
Cover and page design: Becky Daum
Content Consultant: Alexandra Stern, Associate Director of the Center for the History of Medicine, University of Michigan

Library of Congress Cataloging-in-Publication Data
Hall, Margaret, 1947-
  The Panama Canal / M.C. Hall.
    p. cm. — (Events in American history)
  Includes bibliographical references and index.
  ISBN 978-1-60694-450-9 (alk. paper)
  1. Panama Canal (Panama)—History—Juvenile literature. I. Title.
  F1569.C2H356 2010
  972.87'503—dc22

                                2009018094

Printed in the USA

ROURKE PUBLISHING

www.rourkepublishing.com · rourke@rourkepublishing.com
Post Office Box 643328 Vero Beach, Florida 32964

Table of Contents

Chapter One

The First Attempt

The men forced their way through the **tropical** undergrowth. It was hot and humid. Some slapped at mosquitoes. Others were so weak they could barely walk. What were they doing in the jungles of Panama?

It was 1880 and the men were there to build a **canal**. People had been dreaming of this project for centuries.

More than 350 years earlier, Vasco Nuñez de Balboa traveled across Panama after hearing stories about a great body of water. In September 1513 Balboa reached the Pacific Ocean. He claimed it for Spain.

It was not long before people talked of building a waterway to link the Atlantic Ocean in the east to the Pacific in the west. Panama is located on a strip of land called an **isthmus**. At the narrowest point, the two oceans are only 50 miles (80 kilometers) apart.

Explorers found dense jungles when they first visited Panama.

MAGELLAN

Ferdinand Magellan, a Portuguese explorer, reached the Pacific Ocean in the winter of 1519 to 1520. He was the first to do so by sailing around the southern tip of South America.

Without such a waterway reaching the Pacific Ocean from Europe was difficult. Ships had to travel around the tip of South America. The voyage was long and dangerous. Still, centuries passed without anyone building a canal.

In 1849 a group of U.S. businessmen built a railroad across the isthmus. Ships took passengers and freight to the east coast of Panama. Trains carried the people and goods across the isthmus. Then other ships finished the voyage to ports on the Pacific Ocean. Building the railroad proved to be difficult and expensive. However, by 1855 the trains were running.

The idea of a canal was not forgotten. Another canal, the Suez, opened in 1869. This canal linked the Red and the Mediterranean seas through Egypt, a country in northern Africa. A Frenchman named Ferdinand de Lesseps was responsible for building the Suez Canal. Now Lesseps wanted to build a canal in Central America.

Explorer Vasco Nuñez de Balboa crossed the Panama isthmus to the Pacific Ocean in 1513.

Ferdinand de Lesseps made the first attempt to build a canal across Panama.

The Paris Geographical Society set up a committee to study the idea. Lesseps led the committee. French engineers went to Central America to study and map the land.

At the time Panama belonged to the country of Colombia, which was created when Spain gave up its empire. Before a canal could be built, France needed approval from the Colombian government. In 1878 France was given the right to build a canal along the route of the Panama Railroad.

In 1879 the world's best engineers held a conference. Some argued that the canal should be built in Nicaragua.

TROPICAL DISEASE

In the 1880s, doctors were not sure what caused tropical diseases such as malaria and yellow fever. They did not know these diseases were spread by mosquitoes, and treatments were few. Half of those who came down with yellow fever died. Malaria killed even more people. Largely because of these diseases, almost 20,000 lives were lost during the nine years France worked on the canal.

The distance between the coasts was longer than in Panama, but construction would be easier because the land was much flatter.

Lesseps and others wanted to build in Panama. In the end their plan was approved. Lesseps was put in charge of the project.

His first task was to raise money. For a while, Lesseps had trouble getting **investors**. Then he made a trip to Panama to build support.

The French left their equipment behind in Panama when they gave up on their canal project.

He was able to convince thousands of investors to buy shares in his company.

When work started in 1880, one important matter had not yet been settled. Should the canal be dug so the entire length was at sea level? Or should **locks** lift and lower ships along the way?

The Suez Canal was at sea level. It was 100 miles (160 kilometers) long. Lesseps also wanted to build the Panama Canal at sea level. It would only have to be 50 miles (80 kilometers) long. However, some engineers disagreed. They pointed out that the Suez Canal was built across flat, sandy land. Panama was rocky, with steep hills and valleys. In the end Lesseps got his way. The canal would be built at sea level without locks.

Work went very slowly. There were constant problems. Landslides slowed the work and killed or injured workers. Panama's eight-month rainy season caused delays. The twisting Chagres River flooded frequently. Tropical diseases weakened or killed many workers.

Lesseps finally admitted that locks were needed. Unfortunately his decision came too late. In February 1889 the company ran out of money.

Work on the canal ended. It looked like there might never be a passage between the two oceans.

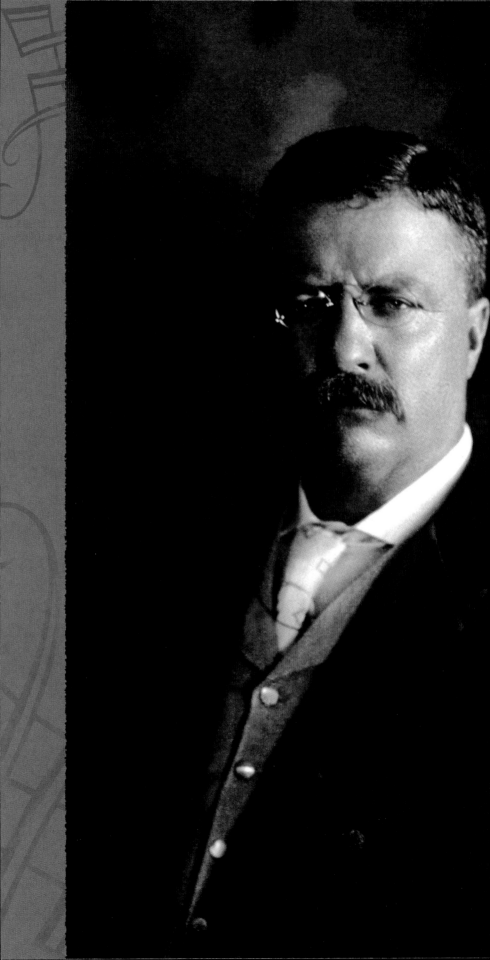

Chapter Two

New Leadership

F rance was forced to give up on digging a canal in Panama. The French left behind buildings, rusty machinery, and piles of dirt. For more than ten years nothing happened.

People continued to talk about linking the Atlantic and Pacific oceans. A canal across Central America still seemed like the best way to do so.

Meanwhile the United States was facing bigger problems. In 1861 the Civil War started. The bloody fighting went on for four years. When the war ended the government's most important job was bringing the country together again.

In 1898 the country faced another conflict. It involved Cuba, an island in the Caribbean Sea. The United States supported Cuba's fight to gain independence from Spain. Naturally this angered the Spanish government.

President Theodore Roosevelt led the United States' effort to build the canal.

WAR PRIZE

After the Spanish-American War the United States took control of the Philippine Islands, in addition to Cuba and Puerto Rico. The Philippine Islands are located in the Pacific Ocean near Japan. They are about 7,000 miles (11,300 kilometers) away from the West Coast of the United States.

The United States sent a battleship called *Maine* to Cuba. In February the ship blew up in the harbor, killing more than 200 U.S. sailors. The United States blamed Spain for the explosion. Within months the two countries were at war.

The Spanish-American War did not last long. In December the United States and Spain signed a peace treaty. Spain turned over control of its territories in the Pacific Ocean and the Caribbean to the United States.

Now there was an even greater need to link the two oceans. President William McKinley set up a group called the Isthmian Canal Commission (ICC) to study the idea of a canal in Central America.

France wanted to sell its rights in Panama to the United States. However, the ICC did not want to build in Panama. It issued a report in 1901. It stated that the best route for a canal was through Nicaragua. President McKinley and many others supported this plan.

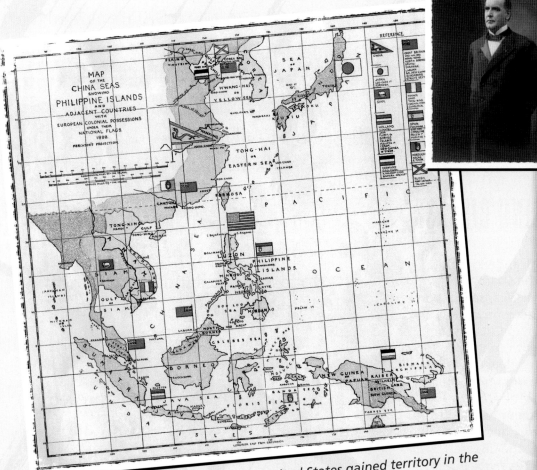

President William McKinley wanted to build a canal through Nicaragua.

After the Spanish-American War, the United States gained territory in the Pacific Ocean, making a canal even more important.

Everything changed on September 6, 1901. President McKinley was shot and killed. Vice President Theodore Roosevelt became president. Roosevelt wanted to take advantage of the work France had already done. He favored building the canal in Panama. Many engineers agreed. In the end Congress voted to build in Panama.

There were still problems to solve before work could begin. Years earlier the United States had signed a **treaty** with Great Britain. Both countries promised not to work alone to build a canal. A new treaty was signed. Great Britain agreed that the United States could build a canal on its own. The United States promised that the canal would be open to all nations.

Now the United States needed permission from Colombia, which still controlled Panama. The United States offered to pay 10 million dollars for the land. It would pay another $250,000 each year. Colombia said no.

President Theodore Roosevelt was angry. He knew that the people of Panama were not happy about being controlled by Colombia. In 1903, Panama declared its independence. President Roosevelt decided to support Panama against Colombia. The United States sent warships to wait in case Colombia decided to fight to keep Panama.

Colombia gave in. On November 3, 1903 Panama became an independent nation. The United States was given rights to a 10-mile (16-kilometer) strip of land across the

This cartoon criticizes the way Roosevelt dealt with Colombia in order to build the canal.

HELD UP THE WRONG MAN

U.S. work on the Panama Canal began in 1904.

isthmus. It was called the Canal Zone. The United States agreed to pay Panama what it had offered Colombia. A lot of Panamanians were unhappy about the treaty. Some wanted more money from the United States. Even so the new government approved the plan. In 1904 the United States paid France 40 million dollars. In return the United States received machinery and buildings the French had left behind in Panama. At last the United States was ready to build a canal.

Chapter Three

Dirt and Disease

Theodore Roosevelt was eager to get started on the Panama Canal. He chose an experienced railroad man named John Wallace as chief engineer. Wallace faced many problems. A lot of the buildings and machines left behind by the French needed repair. Wallace had trouble getting supplies and equipment. Some U.S. workers refused to stay because the living conditions were so poor.

In addition there were problems with the canal itself. The plans called for building a dam and using locks to raise and lower ships through the canal. However, Wallace could not find a good place to build the dam. So he decided a canal at sea level was a better idea.

In June 1904 President Roosevelt sent army doctor William Gorgas to the Canal Zone. Death from tropical diseases was one reason France had failed. Roosevelt did

Landslides slowed work on the canal. This landslide blocked the canal completely until workers removed the extra dirt.

not want the United States to fail for the same reason. Gorgas's job was to prevent tropical diseases such as yellow fever and malaria.

Since France tried to build a canal, scientists had learned a lot about tropical diseases. Now they knew mosquitoes spread yellow fever and malaria. Gorgas planned to solve the problem by getting rid of mosquitoes as he had done during the Spanish-American War.

John Wallace and others, including some members of the U.S. Congress, did not believe that mosquitoes had anything to do with spreading disease. Many felt that Gorgas's work was a waste of money. As a result Gorgas had trouble doing his job.

Late in 1904 there was an outbreak of yellow fever in Panama. A number of people died. Some U.S. workers did not want to risk getting sick so they left for home. Work on the canal almost came to a stop.

Then John Wallace quit his job as chief engineer. On July 1, 1905

CANAL WORKERS

Getting enough workers was a constant problem. Panama had a very small population. Most workers had to come from other countries. There were about 5,000 U.S. workers in the Canal Zone. Far more workers came from Barbados, Martinique, and other islands in the Caribbean. After 1906 some workers also came from Europe.

John Stevens made important progress on the canal before he quit in 1907.

Digging the canal was hard work. Laborers suffered from poor living conditions and disease while building the canal.

President Roosevelt appointed John Stevens to take Wallace's place.

Stevens supported the effort to rid the Canal Zone of mosquitoes. Mosquitoes lay their eggs on the surface of standing water. So Gorgas had his workers drain the swamps. They also spread thin coats of oil on any remaining standing water to kill the young insects. The underbrush along the canal was cut back. Windows were screened to keep mosquitoes out. Roads were paved to get rid of puddles where mosquitoes could lay eggs.

All canal workers were not treated equally. Most U.S. and European workers were white and had the better jobs. They supervised the laborers or worked behind desks. Most laborers were black people from the Caribbean. They carried out the strenuous manual labor. Black workers had much poorer living conditions, too. Their food was prepared in dirty pots in sheds with earthen floors. As a result black workers were three times more likely to die from disease.

Soon yellow fever almost disappeared in Panama. There were also far fewer cases of malaria.

John Stevens was a better leader than Wallace. Stevens realized that getting supplies where they were needed was very important. He also realized that the Panama Railroad was the best way to move supplies. Stevens improved the tracks so heavier loads could be carried. He came up with a system to move dirt and rocks out of the canal. He improved workers' living conditions.

Stevens was also responsible for one of the most important decisions about the canal. He convinced Congress that a system of dams and locks was needed.

It looked like real progress would finally begin. Then with no real explanation, John Stevens quit in 1907. Theodore Roosevelt was forced to appoint a third chief engineer.

This time the president chose George Goethals, an army officer. Roosevelt gave more power to the

George Goethals oversaw the Panama Canal project after John Wallace and John Stevens both quit.

William Gorgas prevented outbreaks of yellow fever and malaria in Panama.

third chief than he had to either Wallace or Stevens. Goethals became president of the Panama Railroad Company and head of the Isthmian Canal Commission. He reported directly to the President. Goethals was highly qualified for the job. People continued to wonder. Could he succeed when two other experienced engineers had given up?

"No single great material work which remains to be undertaken on this continent is as of such consequence to the American people. . . ."

—Theodore Roosevelt, on the building of the Panama Canal

Chapter Four

A Huge Task

George Goethals had his work cut out for him. The canal would be built across the narrowest part of the isthmus. Even so it was a huge job. It included three major construction projects: the Gatún Dam, the Culebra Cut, and the locks.

The Gatún Dam would control the Chagres River. This river twisted its way from the mountains in central Panama to the Atlantic Ocean. During Panama's long rainy season the Chagres could flood in a matter of hours. A dam would block the river, creating a huge lake.

The first step was to change the flow of the river to create a work zone. Workers from France had already dug two new channels and part of a canal so the river flowed four different ways. Now workers built walls of rock and earth to stop the river. They left just one channel open. Then workers cleared the land where the lake would be.

Laborers caused explosions in order to move huge amounts of dirt quickly.

At last they began building the dam. The dam was made from material that had been dug out for the canal. This rock and dirt was dumped on the site one layer at a time. The weight of each new layer pressed down on the layer below it. In time the earth became as hard as **concrete**. Water from the river would back up behind the dam to create Gatún Lake. It would be the largest man-made lake in the world.

At the same time workers were digging out the Culebra Cut. A cut is a large, man-made ditch. The canal would run through the Culebra Cut to Gatún Lake. So the water level in the cut had to be the same as the water level in the lake. The water also had to be deep enough for large ships. That meant the cut had to be huge. It had to be 9 miles (14.5 kilometers) long and 45 feet (14 meters) deep.

Workers from France started the Culebra Cut, but they had made little progress when French work stopped. However, U.S. work crews

Each lock is taller than a six-story building.

Water spills over the Gatún Dam into Gatún Lake.

had better tools to use. One of these tools was **dynamite**. Workers drilled holes and filled them with dynamite. When the dynamite exploded the rocks broke apart.

U.S. workers also had huge steam shovels. These machines loaded the rock onto train cars. The trains carried the rock out of the cut to be dumped.

Panama's long rainy season meant that laborers were usually working in mud. It also meant that landslides were common. In a matter of seconds a slide could bury an area that had taken weeks to dig out. To reduce the chance of landslides the cut was made much wider than planned. This did not end the landslides, but it did make them less of a problem.

Building the locks was one of the biggest jobs of all. They would be made of concrete. At the time concrete had never been used to build anything so large.

The plan called for three sets of locks. Each lock resembled a square box with steel gates at both ends. Each one would be taller than a six-story building!

The first step for the workers was to clear the land where the locks were being built. Then huge molds were made from steel. Workers mixed sand, gravel, cement, and water to make concrete. They used machines and huge buckets to pour

At the time the locks were the largest concrete structures ever built.

the wet concrete into the molds. When the concrete dried, the molds were removed.

Large pipes were also built to carry water to the locks. When the gates at one end were opened water would flow through pipes to fill the lock. To let the water out, the gates at the other end would be opened. Each lock in the canal had two side-by-side sections. That way two ships could go through at the same time. The two ships could travel in the same direction or in opposite directions.

Thousands of men worked on these projects and others. They worked day and night for years. Would the canal ever be finished?

Chapter Five

Linked at Last!

In May 1913 two steam shovels met in the middle of the Culebra Cut. Workers had finally finished digging the huge ditch! Now all that was left to do was to remove dirt and rocks that had fallen into the cut.

In June the last gate on the Gatún Dam spillway was closed. The lake had been filling up slowly. Now the water could rise even higher.

In August a group of people gathered at a set of locks on the Pacific end of the canal. Workers blew up a small dam that had kept the ocean away from the work zone. Water began to flow into the locks. Not long after, the same thing happened on the Atlantic side of the canal.

The United States now had a new president, Woodrow Wilson. In October Wilson pressed a button from Washington D.C. This was a signal to blow up the last dam keeping water out of the Culebra Cut.

The canal cuts through the jungles of Panama.

GATÚN LAKE

Gatún Lake covered many square miles of land, including places where villages had been located. The people who lived in those villages were forced to move. The lake also covered much of the Panama Railroad. The tracks were moved before the lake was filled.

People cheered as water poured into the huge ditch. Now water from both oceans could flow into the canal system. It took months for the canal to fill completely. During that time, workers put the finishing touches on the canal. Every part of the system was tested and retested.

U.S. steam shovels move dirt to complete the Culebra Cut.

Woodrow Wilson was president when the canal was finished.

On January 7, 1914 a ship called the *Alexandre La Valley* entered the canal. The *Alexandre* was an old French crane ship that the United States had used when building the canal. Now it became the first oceangoing ship to travel from one ocean to the other through the canal.

August 15, 1914 was set as the date for the grand opening of the canal. Organizers began planning a celebration. U.S. warships would sail from the United States to Panama for the event. President Wilson planned to be onboard with other important officials.

The ships would sail through the canal from the Atlantic side to the Pacific side. Then they would continue on to an international fair being held in San Francisco, California.

However, these plans changed quickly. On August 1 World War I started in Europe. Although the United States did not enter the war until 1917, no one was in the mood for a celebration.

The canal did open for business on August 15, but the event was a simple occasion. A ship named the *Ancon* became the first to officially travel through the canal. The U.S. president was not onboard. However, the president of Panama and other local officials were.

George Goethals did not sail on the *Ancon*. Instead, he rode alongside the canal in a train car to follow the progress of the ship.

The *Ancon*'s journey was just the beginning for the Panama Canal. Within ten years thousands of ships were traveling through the waterway each year. The oceans were linked at last.

The ship Ancon makes the first official voyage through the canal.

CROSSING THE PANAMA CANAL

From the Caribbean Sea, a ship enters the canal at Limon Bay. It sails at sea level to the first set of locks, the Gatún Locks.

The ship enters the first set of three locks. Water flows into the lock. As the level of the water rises, so does the ship. Each lock raises the ship a little higher. By the time the ship leaves the first set of locks it is 85 feet (26 meters) above sea level.

Then the ship sails into Gatún Lake. It travels across the lake. Then it enters the Culebra Cut, which is now called the Gaillard Cut. It sails on until it reaches another set of locks.

The ship enters the second set of locks. This time water is let out. As the water level gets lower, so does the ship. The gate opens and the ship sails into another lake.

At the far end of the lake the ship enters the third and last set of locks. These locks gradually lower the ship back down to sea level. Then the ship sails through the last section of the canal to the Pacific Ocean.

Locks raise ships above sea level so they can pass through the canal. Gatún Lake is at the center.

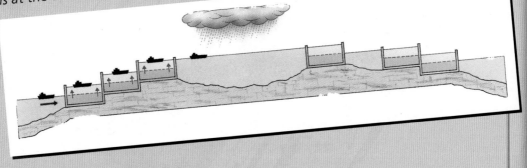

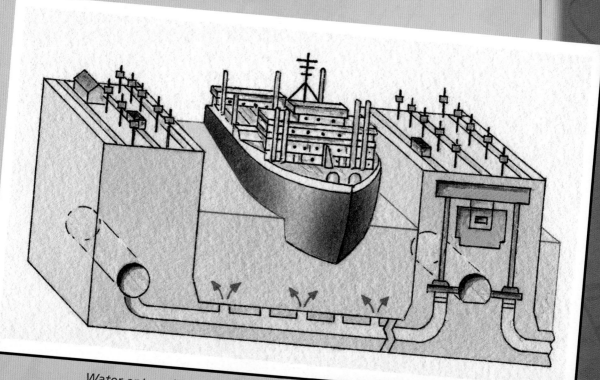

Water enters the lock chambers from below and raises the ships.

Chapter Six

The Story Continues

There was no doubt that the canal was a success. The shortcut between the oceans made it cheaper and faster for countries to trade goods.

The canal also benefited the **economy** of Panama. It provided jobs and helped businesses grow in the region. Many tourists also came to see the canal. They spent money during their visits.

Still, many Panamanians were unhappy that the United States controlled the canal. The Canal Zone was set up so that the United States received much of the profit from the canal. Panamanians staged riots. They tried to take control of the Canal Zone in 1947 and 1964. Each time, people from both nations were injured or killed.

In the 1970s President Jimmy Carter and officials from both the United States and Panama met. They were

Even very large, modern ships are able to pass through the Panama Canal. However, the largest ships are too wide to fit.

CANAL TOLLS

Ships pay tolls to travel through the Panama Canal. The toll depends on the type of ship and on its weight. The money is used to pay for the costs of running the canal.

In 2008 a Disney cruise ship paid a toll of more than $300,000. In 1928 Richard Halliburton paid only 36 cents to make the same trip. However, he swam the entire length! The toll was based on his weight.

determined to come up with a different treaty.

On September 7, 1977 the Panama Canal Treaty was signed. In this agreement the United States gave back most of the land and buildings in the Canal Zone. It also promised to turn over control of the Canal Zone to Panama by the end of 1999. December 31, 1999 was a historic day

The system of locks allows two ships to pass through the canal at once.

President Jimmy Carter (far left) looks on as the new Panama Canal Treaty is signed in 1977.

in Panama. The nation took control of the canal that ran through its center.

Although the canal continues to be important to international travel, things have changed. In the century after the canal opened ships became larger and larger. Many modern ships were too wide to go through the Panama Canal. As a result business began to slow down.

Officials in Panama began to study the idea of enlarging the canal. The project would be very expensive, and it would take years to complete.

Today the Panama Canal provides jobs for about 9,000 people. It operates 24 hours a day, every day of the year.

In 2006 the government approved a plan for expansion. Then the people of Panama had their say. They voted to approve the project.

The final plan involved adding another set of locks that modern ships could use. Work began on September 3, 2007. People came from around the world to celebrate the groundbreaking ceremony.

Spectators lined the edges of the canal to watch the first ship pass through in 1914.

Today, thousands of ships pass through the Panama Canal every year.

When construction is complete in 2014 or 2015, the canal will be able to handle twice as much traffic. The canal will continue to be an important link between two mighty oceans.

"We all know about those who risked so much and tried so hard to build the Canal more than 100 years ago. As we dig, as we build, as we expand the Canal, we will be thinking of those pioneers while also looking to the future."

—Alberto Zubieta, leader of the Panama Canal Authority, as the canal expansion project began

Biographies

Vasco Nuñez de Balboa (1475?–1519)

Around 1500 Balboa explored parts of the Caribbean and Venezuela. In 1513 he led an expedition to the western coast of Panama. He became the first European to see the Pacific Ocean. He was executed for treason in 1519.

George Goethals (1858–1928)

George Goethals was a U.S. Army officer. In 1907 he became the third chief engineer of the Panama Canal project. Under his leadership the canal was finished ahead of schedule. Goethals served as the first governor of the Canal Zone.

William Gorgas (1854–1920)

William Gorgas was a doctor in the U.S. Army. In 1904, Gorgas was sent to Panama to fight yellow fever and malaria. In 1914 he was named Surgeon General of the Army. He continued to work on disease prevention until his death in 1920.

Ferdinand de Lesseps (1805–1894)

Ferdinand de Lesseps designed the Suez Canal. After years of work on the Panama Canal, his company failed. In 1893 he was fined and given a prison sentence for his poor management. However, Lesseps died a year later without serving time in jail.

Theodore Roosevelt (1858–1919)

Theodore Roosevelt was a Spanish-American War hero. In 1901 he became president when William McKinley was assassinated. Roosevelt wanted to build a canal in Central America. He was also interested in conservation and set aside large areas of land in the United States for national parks and monuments.

John Stevens (1853–1943)

In 1905 Stevens became the second chief engineer of the Panama Canal. He was involved in the decision to build the canal with locks. In 1907 Stevens resigned. He continued to work in the railroad industry until his retirement.

John Wallace (1852–1921)

In 1904 John Wallace was appointed chief engineer of the Panama Canal project. Wallace had years of experience as a railroad man and an engineer. However, he had little success in Panama. In 1905 Wallace resigned as chief engineer.

Timeline

1513
Spanish explorer Vasco Nuñez de Balboa is the first European to reach the Pacific Ocean. He claims the ocean for Spain.

1855
The Panama Railroad is completed. It carries thousands of people across the isthmus until the late 1860s, when a transcontinental railroad is completed.

1878
An agreement between France and Colombia gives the French the right to build a canal across Panama.

1889 ▲
Work on the Panama Canal comes to a stop after Lesseps's company runs out of money.

1869
Under the direction of Ferdinand de Lesseps, the Suez Canal is completed. The canal links the Red Sea and the Mediterranean Sea.

1850
U.S. businessmen begin work on a railroad line across the isthmus of Panama.

1846
Colombia and the United States sign a treaty that grants the U.S the right to move people and goods across Panama.

1898
The Spanish-American War ends. The United States gains control of territories in the Pacific and Caribbean.

1879
An international conference is held in Paris, France. Engineers discuss plans for a canal in Central America. Ferdinand de Lesseps is put in charge of the canal.

1903
Panama declares its independence from Colombia.

1904
Doctor William Gorgas comes to Panama to try to rid the region of tropical diseases spread by mosquitoes, such as yellow fever and malaria.

October 10, 1913
Dikes built to hold back water during the building of the canal are blown up. The Culebra Cut begins to fill with water.

September 7, 1977 ▼
The Panama Canal Treaty is signed.

1999
Panama takes over control of the Panama Canal Zone.

January 7, 1914
A French crane boat being used by the United States is the first oceangoing ship to sail through the Panama Canal.

June 27, 1913
The Gatún Dam is completed. Its gates are closed, and water fills the lake.

1904
A treaty between the new government of Panama and the United States is approved. The United States purchases the rights to a strip of land on which a canal can be built.

2006
The Panamanian people vote to approve enlarging the Panama Canal. Work begins in 2007.

August 15, 1914 ▼
The Panama Canal officially opens for business.

Glossary

canal (kuh-NAL): a waterway dug across land

concrete (KON-kreet): a mixture of sand, small stones, cement, and water; used to construct buildings, roads, and other structures

dynamite (DYE-nuh-mite): a material that explodes with great force

economy (i-KON-uh-mee): the system by which a nation produces and uses money and goods

investors (in-VEST-urs): people who provide money to a business in hopes of making more money

isthmus (ISS-muhss): a narrow strip of land that connects two larger areas of land

locks (LOKS): part of a waterway used to lift or lower ships to different water levels

spillway (SPIL-way): a passage for water to flow over a dam

treaty (TREE-tee): a formal agreement between two groups; often meant to keep peace between conflicting parties

tropical (TROP-uh-kuhl): having to do with the tropics. The tropics are hot, wet regions near the equator.

Websites

Live Webcams of Panama Canal Activities
www.pancanal.com/eng/index.html

Make the Dirt Fly!
Smithsonian Museum Exhibit
www.sil.si.edu/Exhibitions/Make-the-Dirt-Fly/blast-1.htm

The Panama Canal Authority
"How It Works"
www.pancanal.com/eng/general/howitworks/index.html

The Panama Canal Museum
www.canalmuseum.com

Reference Map

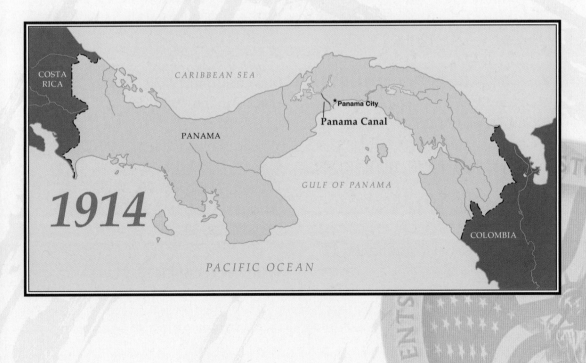

Index